AF351643

SOMEWHERE OVER THE RAINBOW WHERE DREAMS COME TRUE

Teresa Lewis

Somewhere Over the Rainbow Where Dreams Come True

All rights reserved

Copyright © 2023 by **Teresa Lewis**

No part of this publication may be reproduced, distributed, or transmitted in any form or by any means, including photocopying, recording, or other electronic or mechanical methods, without the prior written permission of the publisher, except in the case of brief quotations embodied in critical reviews and certain other noncommercial uses permitted by copyright law.

Published by BooxAi

ISBN: 978-965-578-737-5

SOMEWHERE OVER THE RAINBOW WHERE DREAMS COME TRUE

TERESA LEWIS

CONTENTS

ACKNOWLEDGMENTS

Dear family and friends, I hope you enjoy these poems that I have written over the years. They are about things that were in my life and how I was feeling at the time.

That is what inspired me to write. I hope you enjoy reading them. Some happy, some sad, but at the end of the day my dream finally came true.

They may not make any sense to you, but it was how I was feeling at the time.

Love Always,
Always Have,
Always Will,
Always Do.

Teresa Ann Lewis

"FOR WHAT YOU HAVE DONE"

You have destroyed everything with what you have done.
Your family and friends, and it cannot be redone.
Hurt feelings and no forgiveness for what you have done.
No punishment.
Not good enough for what you have done.
And now they are saying it has all been done.
Free as a bird to spread your wings.
Feel free to come and go as you please.
Not binding by locks or keys.
You have destroyed everything.
With what you have done.
No forgiveness.
No pride in what you have done.
No, I am sorry.
Or please forgive me for what you have done.

"SPEAK YOUR MIND"

Speak those words you have been dying to say.
Pain only hurts for one more day.
Tell it like it is if the truth hurts, by letting the words get in the way.
Be kind.
But nobody is kind to you, so why not be cruel just like they are to you?
Speak those words you have been dying to say, but you put your head
between your legs as they walk away.
Speak those words you have been dying to say.
Maybe the pain will finally go away, but you are too good for that.
You let your heart get in the way and never say the words you have wanted
to say.

"AMANDA"

From the moment the nurse brought you to me all bundled up like a burrito, I did not know what to do. So, I uncovered you to see what it was all about. And all I could see was ten little fingers and ten little toes. And that is when I knew neither your dad nor I knew what to do. Amanda would cry until I held her in my arms. And that is when I knew a baby girl was born. With so much blonde hair and her beautiful blue eyes too.

Amanda means: Worthy of love.

And that is when I knew, as years went by, I was always missing you. Whether I was near or far. I never stopped loving you, Amanda. I hope your dreams will always come true. In the end, there will never be another you. You will always be my little girl. And that is when I knew that not a day would go by that.
Never stop loving you.

"DELAYNA"

A birthday poem for my little girl.
Her hair is yellow as gold, and her eyes the color of blue.
When she smiles at you, she melts your heart as well as the funny things
she says to you.
Delayna Means: Challenger
Delayna, you are my pride and joy and my last miracle.
My life would not be complete if we did not have you bubbling and
bouncing all over the place.
You are like a boomerang.
You cannot stay in one place.
You will always be my baby girl, even when you are all grown up.
And out of this place.

"MISSING YOU"

From the day you left us all sad and blue.
Not letting us say goodbye or even we love you.
Now that you are gone.
I am not going to cry.
I am just going to remember the twinkle in your eye.
Grandpa, I love you.
I always have and I always will.
I wish now I would have come around more often.
And seeing you now that you are gone, I am really missing you.
I miss your smile and your hugs too.
Now I have no grandma or grandpa there in heaven above.
Looking down on you know I am all sad, lonely and blue, not a day goes
by that I do not think about you.

"OUR SONG"

We got married on that September day.
You were standing at the altar, wanting to run away.
Then the music came on.
It played our song.
I crossed my heart, and you said yes.
Anyways, 18 years later, we had a boomerang and a spitfire.
Whoever knew that night at the gas station would have created so many
fires when all you had to do was run away and never look back.
On that very day, a life without you would be a mistake.
Not one day goes by that I do not want to be without you.
We may argue, fuss and fight, but I would not be anything if I did not
have you in my life.

"MY LITTLE SPITFIRE"

Zakary was born.
On a January day, he got stuck and would not come out all the way.
A spitfire from day one.
Now life has begun.
Zakary means: Love and laughter.
He used to be mama's boy, but now he is all grown up playing video
games in his room and never wants to come out.
Today, you turn ten.
And now double digits.
But one of these days, you are going to be a man.
But my spitfire, you will always be.
This miracle of life belongs to me.
Who knew there would one day be a Zakary?
My little spitfire, you will always be.

"MY BEST FRIEND (JO)"

You came into my life that one Halloween night.
And ever since, we have been two peas in a pod.
You were there for me when no one else would be.
You have even been there to comfort me.
I call you my friend.
You can see our meeting that night was meant to be best friends.
That is what you are to me.
You gave up your life just to come to help me.
And no matter what, you are always there for me. You always listen and
never judge me.
A best friend to me, you will always be.
I think about you each and every day.
Sometimes, I bet I drive you crazy.
I hope you will never get rid of me.
A best friend, you will always be to me.
I hope you can see that this life when we met was meant to be a best
friend for me.
You will always be.
I hope you will never have a life without me.

"THIS MEANING OF LIFE"

Love happens around the clock.
You do not have to rush it.
It will happen if it is love.
The meaning of love.
Love one another as if your day were going to end.
Show each other the meaning of love by opening a door or even holding hands.
Give a little kiss on the cheek to show you care.
But if you do not, do not you dare.
This meaningful love is a special thing, and you do not want anyone to get hurt, so if you love to make sure it is the real thing, you will find the true meaning of love in the end.

"YOU'RE GOING TO MISS ME WHEN I'M GONE "

They say you are going to miss me when you are gone, but what happens
if I do not?
And the skies turned to black clouds and lightning?
No happiness, no ray of sunshine only.
Screaming and hollering to get you through your day.
You already know you can do it, and that is your way.
So, no more yelling, as you can see, just a big ray of sunshine shining
down on me.
You are going to miss me when I am gone, but as you look back when you
had me…
Face it, you never really cared about me, so when I am finally gone,
realize what you had now that you no longer have me.

"WORDS HURT"

The mean and hateful words that you say.
You say you love me and that you care.
Then why do you talk to me in such a rude way?
Your words are like stakes through my heart.
You cannot take back the mean words you say.
Not as sorry or please, forgive me ever comes your way.
Just rude words and hateful things that you say.
I see now how much you really feel because if you love someone as much
as you say, you would not let the words hurt that way, so maybe one day
the pain will finally go away, and my broken heart will finally mend the
hurtful and mean words that you say.

"I CALL HER DENISE"

She is my best friend.
She is my rock.
She is my one-of-a-kind.
I call you my sister and my friend.
You will always listen to me and then tell me like it is.
I have your back, and you have mine.

We will one day go to the Caribbean and see the Ocean's blue sea.
Unlike Carnival, when we went to see the fish that we never did see.
I hope you are by my side on the next adventure with me.
I call you Denise, a best friend, sister, and a rock you are to me.
You will always be my one-of-a-kind to me.
I am glad we share the same special day, and you became a best friend
to me.

"A NEWFOUND LOVE"

I have known you for three years and we have always wanted to be
together.
But you had her, and I had him.
But now we have each other.
A newfound love.
Let us give it a try to make it work.
Who cares what people say?
A newfound love is you and me.
If I am happy with you and you are happy with me.
It is finally meant to be a newfound love because you I found.
You.
And you found me.
And now we are finally complete, you and me.

"WHEN YOU ARE YOUNG, YOU WANT TO BE OLD"

When you are young, you want to be old. When you are five, you want to be 10 so you can grow big and strong, and you can ride the big roller coasters and be tall enough to ride.

When you are young, you want to be old. When you finally turn 10, you want to be 20, so you do not have to go to school anymore. No more rules, no more homework. Just to be free running. Play.

When you are young, you want to be old. When you finally turn 20, you want to be 40 so you can play with the kids of your own and be a kid like you used to be and not have to worry about life.

When you are young, you want to be old. When you are 40, you want to be 60, so you do not have to work anymore. And you can enjoy life, partying and playing. But then you turn 60 and you wish to be young again because.

Now your life is over, and you wonder where it has all gone. It is only downhill from here. Your childhood, your adulthood, and now you are too old, and you wish you were young again so you can enjoy life, party, and play again.

"LOVE ME LIKE YOU DO"

Love me like you do.
Put your arms around me like you do.
What are you waiting for?
Just touch me like you do.
You used to talk to me for hours on end, but now you hardly talk to me
at all.
Love me like you do.
I can dream about you, but I don't want to dream it's over.
I'm trying to pull away because I know the truth that it may be finally
over.
I'm dreaming of you holding me in your arms so tight and never letting
me go.
Please just love me.
Love me like you used to do.
No more hurt.
No more pain, I have no feelings.
My heart is broken in two and now I finally know what to do: I am
finally leaving you.

"I HAVE NO FEELINGS"

I no longer can feel, you have hurt me so much.

No love, not even a touch.

Just to blame for a life I cannot explain.

I am no longer in love with you.

My heart has been broken into.

There is nothing you can say or do to mend my heart back into.

I think I may finally be over you.

No flowers, no candy.

No. I am sorry for how badly you treated me.

My heart is empty, sad, lonely, and blue. I have no feelings anymore for you.

Because I am finally over you.

When you had me, you did not want me. You only wanted me to go away.

No time for kids or even a wife. Remember? That is what you say. So now I give you your wish, you can finally have a break.

And I will finally go away.

No more hurt, no more pain. I have no feelings.

My heart is broken in two and now I finally know what to do.

I am finally leaving you.

"LOVE ME"

I put my guard down and let you in.
You said you love me, and that is where I begin.
The touch of your hands on my skin.
Your smile, your kiss on my lips.
You like it when I call you daddy.
And I love it when you call me your baby girl and tell me you love me.
I put my guard down and let you in.
I let you touch me.
And now the love begins.
I cannot wait to be in your arms.
So, you can make love to me again, and I can call you daddy and you can call me your baby girl and say you love me again.

"I FELL IN LOVE"

It has only been a week, but you have given me love like no other.
I have had hurt and pain for many years.
But then you came along and showed me I can love another.
And now I fell in love with you.
Your touch and your smile, too. I never want you to go, so you can.
Hold me tight.
Like I have never been held before, even at night.
I fell in love with you, your smile, and the Way.
The Way you make me feel.
I was always told I could not find another.
And then I found you. You have shown me a love like no other.
I have never had this love. Ever.
I fell in love with you, and I never wanted to end.
I cannot get enough of what you are trying to give me with all your kisses
and hugs.
I finally know what it means to have fallen in love with you.

"SO IN LOVE WITH YOU"

The twinkle in your eye when you look at me.
The smile on your face when you smile at me.
Your kiss when you kiss me.
On my cheek. I'm so in love with you, you're all I think about all day and
night I can't wait to see you.
I count the days and the hours because I'm so in love with you.
I can't wait for you to hold me in your arms nice and tight and make love
to me all through the night I never want you to let me go because I am so
much in love with you.

"PITTER-PAT"

We met that one June day.
I saw your eyes and you saw mine.
Then you smiled at me, and I was putty in your hands. You made my
heart go pitter-patter.
Then, when you kissed my neck, that was all she wrote.
A tug on my hair.
And I was like, oh my God, where have you been all my life?
You have given me a love that I just do not get.
I love it when you kiss me and hold me tight and never let me go through
the night.
You touch me in a way.
That as soon as your fingers touch me in a way, it just makes me go pitter-
patter.

"TORN"

You cannot help who you fall in love with.
Torn.
Between two men.
One gives you pain and sorrow, and the other gives you hugs and kisses
and makes you smile torn between.
Which one really loves you?
And which one is going to follow you?
Torn.
Who is going to walk away when you are lonely and sad?
Torn by who's going to make you cry?
Torn.
I just want to be loved.
So, it is time to say bye.
Bye.
To the old and welcome the new because I finally found someone to love
me now that I found you.

"THROUGH THE MOON AND THE STARS"

No matter how far away I am, I love you to the moon and back.
I never left you guys.
I only left him.
I never meant to make you sad.
I will always be, even if you do not want me to be.
I love you through the moon and stars.
You will see, when you are older, why I had to leave.
I never meant to hurt you.
You will see the hurt and pain he caused me and all the hateful things he said to me through the moon and the stars.
I will always be your mom.
That will never change.
Unless you stop loving me.
To the moon and the stars.
It was always meant to be.
Please do not stop loving me with all the hurtful things you said to me.
Always remember I love you to the moon and back.
So, if you look at the moon and the stars, I am only a phone call away.
I will be right here waiting for the phone to ring on any given day.
Always remember, I love you to the moon and back till my dying day.

"PLEASE DON'T LEAVE"

We have been friends for three years.
You are more of a mother than my own mother is.
I love you so much.
Please do not leave me.
I would give my life to protect yours.
You are my rock, my friend.
If I lost you, I would die inside.
I do not want any time to go by that.
You do not talk to me.
You always said you want me to be happy.
Please do not leave me.
Please be my friend.
To the very end.

"I WILL BE GONE ONE DAY"

I will be gone one day, and maybe I will have found my happy place, and I am just wondering when it is all said and done.
Are you going to put roses on my grave?
Are you going to forget about me, like a memory in a book or a picture in a frame?
Here today, gone tomorrow.
Tomorrow is not promised, so remember to live, laugh, and love, because one day I will be gone and hopefully, you will talk to me and wish that I could talk to you back.
I hope that the people who truly did love me did not forget about me like a memory in a book or a picture in a frame.
Because when I was here, you only wanted to give me 5 minutes of your time.
I have always loved you, always have, always will, always do.
But now I am gone, and I am sure you do not know what to do.
So, when you look up at that Big Blue sky, remember to live, laugh, and love.
Because one day, you two will be gone and you are wondering, well, people will put roses on your grave or just remember you like a memory in a book or a picture in a frame.

"ALL OF ME"

All of me loves everything about you
You make me smile when I am sad and blue
You make me happy with everything you do.
I love you through the moon and the stars.
And with every little thing you do
You bring me to tears when you say I love you.
Because you know that I am leaving even if it is not what I want to do
All of me
Is so in love with you, I found a man who is honest and true
I am so glad to be with you
I get lost when I look in your eyes
Because all of me loved all of you with every little thing you do.

"MY WAY"

You may not have liked what I have done or accepted the people who have come and gone.
People who said they were my friends but then talked about me behind my back.
I did it my way.
When I said goodbye, you did not care about me when I was there, so why care now that I went bye-bye.
You gave me so much hurt and so much pain.
I can't believe I am able to stay insane, so I've decided when it's all said and done that I am going to do it my way to the very end.
You may not like me now or you may have never liked me then.
But I did it my way in the end.

"JUST PRETEND"

Just pretend I am holding you, just pretend I am right there with you,
and I will hold you and love you again when I come home.
All day and night, and never let you go, as long as you are by my side just
pretend,
I am still here even though I am missing you.
Because if I did not have you in my life,
I do not know what I would do, so never let a day go by and do not think
that I do not miss you.
Because you do not have to pretend because
I will never stop loving you.

"BROKEN"

I am broken and I do not know what to do.
The sound of music playing and watching tv reminds me of you.
You broke me.
Broke me in two.
I do not know if I will ever trust again and that is because of you.
You promised me forever and that is a lie too.
When you told people lies about me and that is when I knew what you
were through.
I do not understand what I did so wrong, so wrong for you to just walk
away like you did.
You broke me.
Broke me in two when you left me for the other girl.
When all I ever did was even love you.
Broken.
Taking each day second by second, trying to get through.
You destroyed me, I just do not know what to do.
Because I am simply broken, and the reason is because of you.

"IT FEELS SO RIGHT"

*When I met you on Facebook, I was that shy little girl because I was so
broken and blue and then you drove all those miles to see me.
And I knew you were true, it did not matter if it was only for an hour or
even five minutes.
I am so extremely glad I met you.
You touch me like no one else has, so I knew it feels so right when you
wrap your arms around me and hold me tight and when you kiss me
throughout the night.
You listen to me without judging me, even with all my drama and tears.
You give me encouragement that brings a smile to my face.
That is when I knew it feels so right.
I know you cannot tell me you love me because you do not know me yet,
but I know when you do, it is going to feel so right.*

"A NEW CHAPTER"

It is a new chapter in a new relationship that has come into my life.
I love your smile and I love the way you make me laugh.
I love how you brighten my day and no matter how down I am you say
something to brighten my spirits and bring me back to reality.
That life is going to be better.
A new chapter holding you and kissing you is in my future.
You make my life better each time I talk to you.
You treat me like a lady always.
I have never had that before, only been used, abused, and thrown away.
So, I am really starting to love this chapter.
I wonder where this story will go, and I hope it never ends.
Because it has been a long time since I finally had a new chapter and I
hope it never ends.

"YOU MAKE IT EASY"

You came into my life when I was not expecting it.
Showed me attention I have never had.
Took me to a nightclub that I had never been to.
Danced with me even though you said you did not know how to.
You make it easy being who I want to be. I can laugh and be silly with
you and not worry about you running away.
You make it easy for me to fall in love.
You show me how a lady is supposed to be treated, not broken down and
blue.
You make it easy to want to be with you.
I want to hold you in my arms and never let you go.
I dream of you each day and night.
Until I get to see you, I hope you are my soulmate because you make it
easy loving you.

"ANGELS SENT ME YOU"

Angels sent me you when I was sad and blue.
They were looking over my shoulder when they sent me you.
It was meant for me to go on Facebook and find you.
You are meant for me, and I was meant for you.
We make each other laugh so hard and you bring a smile to my face each
time I talk to you.
Angels sent you to me to bring me happiness and laughter again.
I love the touches and the kisses you send tingling down my spine and
when you kiss my neck you drive me up the wall.
Over and over I never want you to stop giving me the love that was made
for me.
Because I do not think I will ever stop loving you.
Angels sent me you for you to love me.
I want to be your pot of gold at the end of the rainbow.
Because if it were not for angels, I would have never met you.
So, I am glad my angel sent me you and your angel sent me.

"I CAN'T LIVE WITHOUT YOUR LOVE AND AFFECTION"

Mercy, mercy, how am I going to survive nine more days without you holding me and kissing me?
I wake up every day knowing that it is only one more day away.
I do not know how I can live without your love and affection.
I do not want to face another night alone; I want your arms around me all the time.
I want you to be the one I come home to every night.
I cannot live without your love and affection.
I want it every day and every night.
You are wrapping your arms around me making sweet love to me.
Only nine more days until I get your love and affection and your back in my arms again.

"GOOD DIRECTIONS"

I was sitting there on a dating site waiting for the right time. Then you
came along and liked my page.
And we started talking and laughing for hours.
Then you made your way up to Ely.
So you could finally meet me.
It must have been good directions that I gave you because you have not
stopped talking to me since day one you met me.
I am so excited when I am around you.
You make me feel like me and not somebody that I used to be afraid to talk
to and be on pins and needles.
I know I can be wild and free when you are with me.
You never make me sad, lonely, or blue because you are always with me.
Even when you are not here, you find a way to make me happy.
So good directions are what I found when I found you.
I just hope you keep going in the same direction and never turn around
because I think I would be lost if one day you decided to turn back around
and go the other way.

"THE WAY YOU MAKE ME FEEL"

The way you make me feel when I am with you is unexplainable.
You make me laugh all the time even when I am not with you. You say
things to make me laugh and smile and that is why I am so into you.
You know how to treat a lady and that is what I like about you.
The way you make me feel when you touch me is like the 4th of July, an
explosion.
And when you smile at me, you melt my heart because I have never had
someone so into me like you.
Is this love?
I think so, because the way you make me feel when I am with you is like
nothing other than I have ever had, so let me be the one you make promises
to.
Because I always want to be the one because of the way you make me
feel.

"TREASURE"

You make me laugh all the time when you smile you melt my heart.
You have an amazing heart that I will treasure.
I love it when you give me attention and we wrestle, and you play jokes
on me.
You make me laugh so hard. I will treasure the memories we have already
had. I hope there is more treasure to come.
I love how you hold me at night and the way you hold my hand and open
the door for me, too.
I treasure you; you are my friend.
I can tell you anything, you mean so much to me, even if you do not know
that.
You have a special place in my heart. I am so excited to wake up in the
morning just to hear your voice.
I treasure you more than words can say.
My whole life has changed since you came into my life. You are my world
and I treasure you with everything.
If you are looking for a woman to treat you right, I'm your treasure and I
hope one day we can treasure each other and make lots of memories to
treasure together always.

"ON MY WAY TO YOU"

I was on my way to you on an abandoned road with no signal just to get to you.
Seven dominos later, I finally found you.
I knew you were the one.
You make me happy, that is why I am on my way to you.
You bring me so much joy and happiness just to hear your voice and when we video chat, I love seeing your smile.
It lights up my day like the 4th of July.
I am on my way to you to say I want you to be my one and only till the day I die.
Thank you for showing me the love I have been longing for my whole life.
I did not think I could love again when I met you.
A romantic gentleman with compassion and caring and laughter and someone who knows how to treat me.
You treat me like a queen, and I want you to be my king till my dying day.
And I cannot wait to be on my way to you.
And give you the love we both need.

"THIS ROAD I'M ON"

*This road I am on has taught me a lot, from the friends that I thought I
had, to the friends that have not.
Only true friends do not stab you in the back.
Only true friends have really got your back.
So, this road I am on has taught me a lot to keep your friends close and
your enemies closer, because you never know who is going to be there for
you in the end and who is not.
The games that people play are going to hurt you in the end, when you see
how much you hurt you in the end. When you see how much you have
broken me and that you are no longer my friend in the end.
This road I am on, we cannot wait until life is not hard anymore before
we decide to be happy.
Life is not always rainbows and butterflies, it is about what is right.
And not stabbing somebody in the back even though you know it does not
feel right.
So, as I said, this road I am on has taught me a lot to really realize who
my real friends are and who are not.*

"A THOUSAND GOODBYES"

*From the time you were born till the time I got to hold you in my arms, I
have loved you.*
*Even though I may or may not have been there, not a day goes by that I do
not think of each and every one of you.*
*I know that you have said goodbye, some have given me another chance.
And some will not even call me to say hello.*
*I miss my children each and every day and not a thousand goodbyes can
keep me from you.*
*I am down but I am not out, it is just going to take me some time to get on
my feet.*
*No matter how many times you push me away I am going to keep trying
to come see you.*
It is going to take a thousand tomorrows.
*I am never going to say goodbye, I am going to keep trying until the day
I die.*

"DEPRESSION"

Depression is real when you have no one to care for or even love you.
Days and nights you are so all alone.
Nobody to see and have nothing to do and your phone does not even ring.
It is like you are a memory that has gone away.
Nobody cares if you are here on any given day.
People say how can you be depressed, all you have to do is keep pushing through and the pain will go away.
I am so depressed, lonely, sad, and blue I am to the point I do not know what to do.
Days and nights go passing by, but your phone never rings.
Even when you feel all alone there is no one to catch you and be a friend in the end.
So, remember people, depression is real and you should always be a friend, a friend in need.

"I DO NOT BELIEVE"

I do not believe in anything anymore.
I do not believe in hopes and dreams, just tears and sorrow.
I do not believe there is a happy ever after.
I do not believe in dreams because they never come true. God says he does
not do things to you that you cannot handle.
I do not believe that is true.
I do believe in love.
I believe in who your true friends are and who is going to stand by your
side and not stab you in the back and then go run and hide.
I do not believe, I do not care what happened yesterday.
I just want to move away when I am gone, nobody is ever going to care
about me anyway.
Yesterday is Yesterday.
Today is a new day.
If you can't let the past go, you just need to walk away because I am not
going to run and hide because I just don't believe.
All the pain you have put me through and caused all my family and
friends to walk away I just don't believe what you did to me.

"LIFE KEEPS MOVING ON"

Nobody cares if you are here or gone, but life keeps moving on, so do not forget to put your big girl pants on and deal with it.
Because life keeps moving on, do not let them stomp all over your heart and your dreams too.
Let them know they cannot get the best of you.
No matter what they try to do, because life keeps moving on with or without you.
Somewhere over the rainbow where dreams come true.
And life keeps moving on because of you.

"BLESS THIS BROKEN ROAD"

Bless this broken road I am on.
I have been put through pain and sorrow and I keep going.
I keep fighting every day and I am not going to quit.
Even though I want to because at the end of the day I am going to put my
shoulders back and hold my head up high, so that nobody can get in my
god damn way.
Bless this broken road that I am on, and all the pain and sorrow that I
have gone through is going to finally set me free and bring me back to you.
People tell you that I do not care and that is not true.
Not a day goes by that I do not miss you.
It is not that I do not want to come and see you.
Bless this broken road that I am on, I need to fix the cracks and potholes
before I can drive down that road again.
Just to be told that I am not good enough and you are not welcome here.
So, one of these days this broken road will be fixed, and I will finally
make my way back to you.

"NOBODY KNOWS"

Nobody knows the hurt and pain you put me through now I am finally over you.
Nobody knows all the times I have cried inside with all the hateful words that you said to me.
When I am not around, you put on a show to make yourself look big when deep down inside you are small.
I am so sad, lonely, and blue because you destroyed my life with everything you do.
Nobody knows all the pain that you have caused me with everything you do.
And that is the reason I am never coming back to you.
And I will never miss you.

"YOU HAD ME FROM HELLO"

*From the moment I met you I knew you were the one. You had me from
hello and now I do not know what to do.
That is why I keep fighting to be with you.
My favorite line was "Will you ever call me again"?
And you said, "Will See."
And then I look in those beautiful blue eyes shining down on me.
And the way you look back at me melts my heart. You had me from hello,
and I am praying one day.
You choose "Pick me and never leave me."
Because it feels so right when you are holding me in your arms, and we
can be complete. You had me from hello, from the 1st kiss I ever received, I
knew I did not ever want it to end.
And I never wanted you to leave because I knew you were the one for me.
So now I will ask this question:
Did I have you from hello?
Like you had me, I guess as time goes by the answer is "will see".*

"IN THE STILL OF THE NIGHT"

*You came 280 miles to come see me, but I must have spooked you because
you went running away from me.
In the still of the night, I lay in bed, and I keep waiting patiently that you
finally one day come back to me and say you love me.
In the still of the night with the moon and the shining bright, I would go
to the end of the earth for you to say you love me tonight.
I want you to be my Harvey and me to be your Donna and I want you to
come one day running back to me and hold me tight and for you to stay.
In the still of the night looking up at the stars.
Thinking about the night that we finally met and me and realizing
something finally went right.
In the still of the night, I was meant for you, and you were meant for me,
and I know it feels right,*

"ALL THROUGH THE NIGHT"

As I lay in bed all through the night looking at you while you are looking at me.
Wondering how someone like you would ever be with someone like me.
All through the night with you laying there peacefully.
I wonder how life ever went right for me with you coming into my life.
They broke the mold when God brought you to me.
You are my knight and shining armor and you always know what to do.
You made me happy again because I was sad lonely and blue.
Those kisses on my eyes drive me crazy and make me go insane.
Just thinking about you by my side it is the only place I ever want to be.
Laying there in your arms and holding me tight and never letting me go all through the night.

"NEVER SAY GOODBYE"

Never say goodbye and that you are ever going to leave me.
I do not like goodbyes, I only like till I see you again.
You say you cannot make a decision you have to go with your heart and
what your head says.
And I hope you pick me in the end.
And never say goodbye to me.
Not a moment goes by that I do not want you near me. The way you make
me laugh makes me who I want to be. I do not have to put on a show, I
can be the real me.
So never say goodbye because I do not ever want you to leave me so in the
end, I can be with you, and you can be with me, and we can finally be
complete.

"TONIGHT, I WANT TO CRY"

Months and months go by, and you finally call me and tell me I have destroyed your life.
Tonight, I want to cry because I do not understand what I did to make you say goodbye.
We were like peas in a pod and now I cannot even get a hi.
Tonight, I want to cry. I just want all the hurt and pain to go away and for you to be by my side.
So tonight, I want to cry, and I did not realize that you were going to say goodbye and never talk to me again on any given day.
Tonight, I want to cry for being sad, lonely, and blue. Now I am all alone and I do not know what to do.
So tonight, I want to cry with tears in my eyes because I am missing you and not a day goes by that I am not thinking about you.

"MY BEST FRIEND" (HELENE)

You came into my life like a ray of sunshine.
You have never judged me.
You have always been my support line.
We have had our ups and downs. But no matter what, you have never left my side.
I call you my best friend, my rock, my ride or die.
Without you in my life I do not know how I can survive.
You make me happy when I am sad, you bring a smile to my face every time we talk.
You give me advice even when I do not take it.
That is why I call you my best friend.
You have always been there for me no matter what the ending outcome is.
That is why I call you my best friend.
I could not imagine my life without you, and I hope we will stay friends till the very end.

"SEASONS"

As the trees change colors and the snow hits the ground.
Not a day goes by that I do not miss you.
Changes happen all through the year
Jan-March is cold. Easter bunny comes in spring and I am always
missing you. May is Mother's Day, thinking of when you guys were born,
then comes summer, June-August, and you are still gone, and you are on
vacation again. Then a new school year starts you become so much
smarter. Then Halloween happens and you go trick or treating then. Along
comes Thanksgiving and turkey day and to give thanks for all you have in
your life.
And a few weeks later it is Christmas to enjoy time with family and
friends. And then suddenly, the year is gone, and a new year has begun.
The seasons stay the same through the year, the only thing that changes are
you not wanting me there. I always want to be there no matter what, I
just need you to show me with a phone call or a text.
I will drop everything I got going on like a drop of a hat just to hear your
voice and to see you again. Hope the seasons change and you come running
back to me. With a phone call or even a text.
I will be waiting for that very day for you to come running back to me.
With a phone call or even a text. I will be waiting for that day for you to
come running back to me.

"WONDER"

I lay in bed, and I wonder if I will ever be anybody first choice or will I always be second.
Wonder: Why I am never good enough to be the one.
Wonder: Will it ever be me that you come running to.
Wonder: If you will ever be going to tell me that my heart belongs to you.
Wonder: What goes through your head when you look at me.
Wonder: How much longer do I need to wait patiently?
Wonder: How long is it finally going to take you to love only me?
Wonder: if it is ever going to be meant to be you and me.
Only time can and "Will see."

"SOMETHING TO BELIEVE IN"

*So, you have been told for 20 years that you are a nothing, a nobody, a
waste of space.
That none of your dreams will ever come true.
One of these days, your dreams will finally come true as long as you keep
believing in the person you are.
You always have something to believe in, even if it never comes true.
But at the end of the day always keep trying no matter how many people
put you down and call you a nothing, a nobody and a loser.
You know it is not true. Hopefully, one day, my kids and my parents will
come back to me, too
So, one of these days, I have something to believe in and that is because
of you,
Always remember and never give up because once you give up
Then you are giving the other person there just desserts,*

*So why not just make your dreams come true and do what you were meant
to do?*

"GOOD OLÉ BOY"

You came into my life 3 years ago. You started as my friend and then became my brother, no blood relation, just accepted me as the good olé boy you are. You are my doctor, lawyer and my therapist. You give me advice even though I did not take it, always listened to me vent and complain over "morning therapy".

And then you tell me like it is. That is why I call you my brother that I can only wish I had. I was born an only child and if anyone wanted a brother, I wish I could have had you in my life.

I would not have been so alone, you cheer me up when I am down. You can always make me laugh with the funny things that come out your mouth. You stay on the phone with me for hours on end. Just to make sure that I am happy again. You are a good olé boy and that is why I call you my brother and my friend. You taught me so much. You taught me the parts of a CDL truck and to make sure and not levitate the seat. And give the poor old man a heart attack and you also taught me if you want something you have to work hard for it, and it will be yours in the end. But most importantly, you never gave up on me, you were always there through the thick and thin.

That is why I call you a Good Olé Boy, my brother, and my friend.

"NEVER GIVE UP"

Never give up on life, you must keep fighting every day.
Keep pushing as if today was your last day.
Never give up no matter what you do.
You deserve that to yourself to do the best that you can do.
Nothing is going to hit you harder in life if you fail, you get right back up
and you are damn sure.
"NEVER GIVE UP"
Because once you do they know they won and what better way to shut
them up.
So, they cannot kick you while you are down.
Because every day you keep getting back up and doing the best you can.
I do not want to fail in life so that is why I never give up.

"DON'T LAUGH AT ME"

You used to laugh at me when I was big as a cow.
Now I am no longer big, I am finally small.
"Don't laugh at me"
Because look who is laughing now, I am finally succeeding in life, and you
wonder how? I did not give up!
Or give you the satisfaction for you to go run your mouth.
That is what you always did make yourself look big
When deep down you are small.
"Don't laugh at me"
I may not have any money then or even now.
I am a millionaire that is what you preach very well.
Look who has all the money and cannot find a woman who will stay by
your side and not duck tail and run and hide. You think because you have
money, I am going to come running back to you, not a chance in hell.
"Don't laugh at me" because look who is laughing now.
When you had me all you did was laugh at me, call me names, belittle
me, and put me down.
Now that I am no longer a part of your life look who is laughing now. So
"do not laugh at me" now because I made it and proved you all wrong.
Because you did not care about me then just like you do not care about
me now.

"WITH OR WITHOUT YOU"

One day my success will finally happen. I will not give up trying until my dreams come true. With or without you, I will prove you wrong one day. When all my dreams have come true. It may not be today or even tomorrow but it will be before I take my last breath on this earth. I am going to fight every day until my dream finally comes my way and I can show the world my talent that has been hidden away and it is finally time for it to soar to the sky.

With or without you I will find a way to make my dreams come true, but when I finally do, remember I am the one you threw away because I was not good enough for you now to come my way when you did not stand next to me during the good times and the bad times. I was not important enough for you to stay so I am not doing it with or without you because in the end you should have never thrown me away and look at me now I can do it with or without you.

I have learned my way.

"WANTING THE BEST FOR YOU"

As the tears go rolling down my face, all I do is think of you guys running and playing all over the place.
Wanting the best for you.
You have been told that I do not want to see you. That is not true.
It is just my pride is getting the best of me.
Afraid I am going to be told to leave and what are you doing here anyway.
I want the best for you, but I want to see you too and I want to hear from you.
A text or a phone call will show me you still care that is why I do not come see you because
I want the best for you, and I am just going to get in the way.
Because if you cared about me, I am only a phone call or a text away.
And nothing ever comes my way, it is like you completely forgot about me, so that is why I stayed away because in the end it does not seem like you cared about me anyway.

"A NOTE TO MYSELF"

When you find someone, you love, love them with all your heart. It does not matter if he is rich or poor, it is how they treat you at the end of the day. Isn't that all that truly matters anyway?

A note to myself

It does not matter what anyone else says because you are not going to listen to them anyway. You are going to listen to your heart and follow your dreams. Because at the end of the day that is the man you truly love, and nobody else's opinion really matters anyway.

A note to myself

If I must wait a week, a month or even a year, I will be right here waiting for you patiently to finally make us complete.

One final note to myself

Make sure the man you fall in love with puts a smile on your face and laughter in your heart. Make sure his heart is so pure and made of gold so one day he will make you the luckiest girl in the world.

"SHE WISHES SHE COULD TURN BACK TIME"

*On a sun shining day a long time ago, there was this boy and this girl,
and they really loved their momma not so long ago.
But their momma was so heartbroken, sad, and blue, and she did not
know what to do, so she left.
Just remember she did not leave because of you, she left it because she was
tired of getting yelled at and being belittled and getting called names too.
And she could not take it anymore, so that is what she had to do.
She wishes she could turn back time and take the boy and the girl with her.
But the boy and the girl wanted to stay, they did not want to leave with
her anyway.
So why blame the momma for doing what she had to do?
The momma left to find herself but every day she wishes she could turn
back time.
Because is she knew then what she knows now, she would have never left
you behind, she would have taken you with her. She wishes she could turn
back time so she could love you again because not so long ago there was a
boy and a girl who really loved their momma in the end and now she is a
distant memory and she doesn't know what to do to get that love that the
boy and girl used to give their momma before she left them behind and the
reason is because of you, now they don't even call her mom anymore it is
only the name she goes by to.*

"TRUE LOVE"

When a man loves a woman and he wants to propose he has a ring, and he gets down on one knee.

He wants to spend the rest of his existence with her unconditionally. That is what true love is, she loves him with all her heart, mind, body and soul. And as soon as she says yes, their love is finally complete, and he is finally giving her his last name because he realized it was true love and she is the one to make him complete. She is standing at the altar wearing all white and he is in a tuxedo.

They are happy as can be because they will be finally complete as one, but then when the Preacher says "Is there anyone that objects to these two people getting married, speak now or forever" hold your peace and so then the Preacher says "by the power vested in me, I know pronounce you husband and wife, you may kiss your bride."

As he reaches in to give her the kiss, she has been waiting for her whole entire life, she closes her eyes for a brief second and then opens her eyes up just to realize she is lying in bed and realizing it is only a dream.

An amazing dream that she had so she goes to the window, and she wishes upon a star to one day be with her one and only true love and they can finally be complete as one.

"I STILL BELIEVE"

I still believe.
I never thought I would find love ever again.
All I ever found was heart break and misery until
The day I found you on a dating site and that is
When I knew you were the one for me.

So, I still believe that there is love out there for me.
You are my knight and shining armor and I cannot wait
To hold you in my arms and for us to be complete.

At the end of the day, I still believe that there is finally love out
For me. And that is really meant to be.
You and me together.
I am so glad that you believe.
That I am the one for you and you are the one for me.

"SHE IS STRONG ENOUGH TO MAKE IT HAPPEN"

There is this hard-working woman that was told she will never
Succeed in life. She is strong enough to make it happen.
She falls on her face more times than she can count, but she gets back up
and tries again.
She has been so far down that at one point she wished God would just
take her to heaven.
So, she would not have to worry about it no more.
No more stress or how to pay bills or how she is going to eat at night and
keep a roof over her head.
She is strong enough to make it happen, she gets back out there, she stands
on her own two feet and makes it happen.
What she is missing more than anything in the world is hearing those
three words and that never happens.
She is missing love and family to call her one again like she used to have
way back when.
Now she has no one to give her the love and attention that she needs and
finally be accepted, which in her family that is never going to happen.
That is why she wished God would just take her to heaven and take care
of all her needs.

"EVERYTHING YOU KNOW IS NOTHING"

This is not how it is supposed to be.
You are never supposed to not include me.
You are always supposed to love me no matter what happens in life.
Everything you know in life is nothing, you are not supposed to throw me away like I did not even matter.
I did not throw you away, I knew whatever I had to say would not matter anyway.
So, what can I do to get you back in my life again and be part of things?
Like it used to be back in the day.
Nothing really matters anymore because I do not have you in my life.
Everything you know is nothing if you do not have a family and someone who loves you in your life.

"SOMEONE TO LOVE ME"

I hope the day will come when someone tells me that they love me again.
And I am not used and abused and made fun of.
Someone to hold me in their arms and hold me tight and never let me go.
For them to say, "I am the best thing in the world that ever happened to
them in the world" and they put me 1st above anything else.
That I am the only thing that matters.
Someone to love is what I am looking for, instead of being lonely and sad.
Something will come about it in their entire life.
Someday, my day will come for me to find my one and only true love,
someone to love and call my own, someone to love is what I am waiting
for.

"PIECE BY PIECE"

The words you say turn my heart to stone. Broken is my heart.
Broken in two with no love from each one of you.
Fighting just to stay alive and put the pieces back together.
Trying to get the love I once had from you.
But there is a barrier in your life that will not let that happen.
And that is why I am so torn into two.
Piece by piece I will put the puzzle back together and make my way back
to you.
No matter how far away I am from you.
Do not think for one day that I ever I ever stopped loving you.
Because piece by piece, I will make it back to you and I will always be
loving you till the very end.

"MISSING PIECE"

You came into my life two years ago.
We have had our ups and downs and at the end of the day.
We have always managed to laugh together.
You are my missing piece and I want it to be permanent for the rest of my
life that I get to live.
You are my missing piece, I would like for you to be my missing piece.
Make me the happiest woman in the world and tell me you will say yes,
and we can be complete.
I want you today, tomorrow, for the rest of my life.
I always have always will always do love you because you are my missing
piece.
We are a great team, we never fight, we work together as one and we are
complete so just say yes and be my missing piece.

www.ingramcontent.com/pod-product-compliance
Lightning Source LLC
Chambersburg PA
CBHW051813130726
47987CB00003B/1239